Log It • My Personal

Password • DeskBook

Email • Organizer

A must have book for Computer Users

Christine (Barea) Ballano

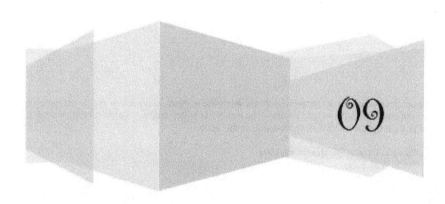

Outskirts Press, Inc.
Denver, Colorado

My Personal Internet Deskbook Organizer
For Those Who Forget
All Rights Reserved.
Copyright © 2009 Christine T. Ballano
V1.0

Outskirts Press, Inc.
http://www.outskirtspress.com

ISBN: 978-1-4327-3422-0

Library of Congress Control Number: 2008943742

Outskirts Press and the "OP" logo are trademarks belonging to Outskirts Press, Inc.

PRINTED IN THE UNITED STATES OF AMERICA

NEVER FORGET
SUPPORT OUR TROOPS

FIGHTING FOR FREEDOM
FOR ONE AND FOR ALL

Ever get Frustrated When You Try To Retrieve Your Password and You have To Have It Sent To The Email Address You Forgot The Password For Too..????

Don't Worry Anymore!

Save It!

      Store It!

           Remember it!

In Your Handy Personal Internet Desk Book Organizer

I dedicate this book

To my senior friends, family and school chums who

Constantly forget or misplace their passwords, user names etc. or

just need someplace to keep track of them.

I hope that this book will simplify their internet, personal and school record keeping.

Table of Contents

Country Codes   1
Travel Info   3
Quick Find Links   4
Time Zones   6
A-Z Personal E-mail Sheets   7
Misc Email Sheet   94
Frequently Called Numbers   96
Class Schedule   98
Things to Do   99
Senior Help   101
Hot Links   102
Important Events   103
Computer Troubleshoot   104
Protect Your Computer   108
Notes   109
Free Medical Clinics   110
2009 Calendar   112
2010 Calendar   113
Holidays and Observances   114
Weights and Measures Conversion Chart   116
Eye Exams and Surgery   118

COUNTRY CODES

AF	Afghanistan	GM	Gambia
AL	Albania	GE	Georgia
DZ	Algeria	DE	Germany
AD	Andorra	GH	Ghana
AO	Angola	GT	Guatemala
AI	Anguilla	ID	Indonesia
AQ	Antiqua & Barbuda	IR	Iran
AR	Argentina	GI	Gibraltar
AM	Armenia	GR	Greece
AW	Aruba	GL	Greenland
AU	Australia	GD	Granada
AT	Austria	GP	Guadeloupe
BS	Bahamas	HK	Hong Kong
BH	Bahrain	HU	Hungary
BD	Bangladesh CO		
	Columbia	BB	Barbados
CR	Cost Rica	BE	Belgium
HR	Croatia	BM	Bermuda
CU	Cuba	BO	Bolivia
CZ	Czech Republic	BA	Bosnia-Herzegovina
DK	Denmark	BR	Brazil
DM	Dominican Republic	BG	Bulgaria
EC	Ecuador	KH	Cambodia
EG	Egypt	CM	Cameroon
SV	El Salvador	KY	Cayman Islands
EE	Estonia	CF	Central Africa
ET	Ethiopia		Republic
FK	Falkland Islands	TD	Chad
FJ	Fiji Islands	CL	Chile
FI	Finland	CN	China
FR	France		

COUNTRY CODES

SA	Saudi Arabia	VI	Virgin Islands (USD
SN	Senegal	YE	Yemen
SG	Singapore	YU	Yugoslavia
SO	Somalia	ZR	Zaire
ZA	South Africa	ZW	Zimbabwe
SU	Soviet Union (former)		
ES	Spain		**Some New Ones**
LK	Sri Lanka		
SD	Sudan	AX	Aland Islands
SR	Suriname	AC	Ascension Islands
SE	Sweden	BJ	Benin
CH	Switzerland	BT	Bhutan
YW	Taiwan, Province of	BW	Botswana
	China	BV	Bouvet Island
TZ	Tanzania	CA	Canada
TH	Thailand	CC	Coco Islands
TT	Trinidad & Tobago	CY	Cyprus
TN	Tunisia	GY	Guyana
TR	Turkey	MR	Mauritania
TC	Turks & Caicos	MD	Muldova
	Islands	MS	Montserrat
UG	Uganda	N	Neutral Zone
UA	Ukraine	NE	Niger
AE	United Arab Emirates	PW	Palau
UK	United Kingdom	PN	Pitcairn
US	United States	PR	Puerto Rico
UY	Uruguay	WS	Samoa
VA	Vatican City State	RS	Serbia
VE	Venezuela	SZ	Swaziland
VN	Vietnam	SY	Syria
VG	Virgin Islands	To	Tonga
	(British)	SU	USSR (former)
		EH	Western Sahara
		ZM	Zambia

Look for us up on **at Sparkysemporium**

SparkysEmporium.com for Vintage/Custom Jewelry

Travel Info

TRAVEL—Put your favorite Travel Sites Here	

Quick Find Links

AARP
http://www.**aarp**.org/

AMAZON
http://www.amazon.com

AMERICAN BAR ASSOCIATION
http://www.abanet.org

BAY 9 AUCTIONS
http://www.bay9.com

CAPITOL ONE
http://www.capitolone.com

CASINO AIR
http://www.casinoair.com

CITIBANK
http://www.**citibank**.com

CVS
http://www.**cvs**.com

CLUB MOM
http://www.clubmom.com

EBAY AUCTIONS
http://www.ebay.com

JET BLUE AIRWAYS
http://www.jetblue.com

KIJII
http://tampabay.kijiji.com

WORLD WIDE YELLOW PAGES
 http://www.Yellow.com

YAHOO
http://www.yahoo.com

MSN
http://www.m.msn.com

LSAC
http://www.os.lsac.org

NALA Campus
www.nala.com

ANCESTRY
http://www.ancestry.com

CLASSMATES
http://www.classmates.co

ELLIS ISLAND
http://www.ellisisland.org

FAMILY HISTORY
http://www.familyhistory.com

SOCIAL SECURITY
www.ussocialsecuritysearch.com

Quick Find Links

For Kids

Neopet	http://www.neopet.com
Upromise	http://wwwUpromise.com

For Seniors

SeniorsvsCrime	http://www.seniorsvscrime.com
Abuse Hotline	http://www.ncea.aoa.gov

Report fraud

Telephone Communications	http://www.fcc.gov
Identity Theft, Debt Collection,	http://www.ftc.gov
Do Not Call Registry and more	

Useful Government Sites

Postal	http://www.usps.com
National Institute of Health	http://www.nih.gov
National Weather Service	http://www.noaa.gov
Treasury Dept.	http://www.ustreas.gov
Navy	http://www.navy.mil
Army	http://www.army.mil

Top Ten Portals

AOL

Yahoo

MySpace

Google

Lycos

Ask Search Network

Blogger

Standard time in the U.S. and its territories is observed within eight time zones. Standard time within each time zone is an integral number of hours offset from a time scale called **Universal Time, Coordinated** (abbreviated UTC), maintained by a large number of very precise "atomic clocks" at laboratories around the world, including the U.S. Naval Observatory.

To obtain U.S. civil time from UTC, use the following table.

Atlantic Daylight Time	subtract 3 hours from UTC
Atlantic Standard Time	subtract 4 hours from UTC
Eastern Daylight Time	subtract 4 hours from UTC
Eastern Standard Time	subtract 5 hours from UTC
Central Daylight Time	subtract 5 hours from UTC
Central Standard Time	subtract 6 hours from UTC
Mountain Daylight Time	subtract 6 hours from UTC
Mountain Standard Time	subtract 7 hours from UTC
Pacific Daylight Time	subtract 7 hours from UTC
Pacific Standard Time	subtract 8 hours from UTC
Alaska Daylight Time	subtract 8 hours from UTC
Alaska Standard Time	subtract 9 hours from UTC
Hawaii-Aleutian Daylight Time	subtract 9 hours from UTC
Hawaii-Aleutian Standard Time	subtract 10 hours from UTC
Samoa Standard Time	subtract 11 hours from UTC

Website:
User Name: _____
PW: _____
http:// _____
Email: _____

Website:
User Name: _____
PW: _____
http:// _____
Email: _____

Website:
User Name: _____
PW: _____
http:// _____
Email: _____

Website:
User Name: _____
PW: _____
http:// _____
Email: _____

Website:
User Name: _____
PW: _____
http:// _____
Email: _____

Website:
User Name: _____
PW: _____
http:// _____
Email: _____

Website:
User Name: _____
PW: _____
http:// _____
Email: _____

Website:
User Name: _____
PW: _____
http:// _____
Email: _____

Website:
User Name: _____
PW: _____
http:// _____
Email: _____

Website:
User Name: _____
PW: _____
http:// _____
Email: _____

Website:
User Name: _____
PW: _____
http:// _____
Email: _____

Website:
User Name: _____
PW: _____
http:// _____
Email: _____

Website:
User Name: _____
PW: _____
http:// _____
Email: _____

Website:
User Name: _____
PW: _____
http:// _____
Email: _____

Website:
User Name: _____
PW: _____
http:// _____
Email: _____

Website:
User Name: _____
PW: _____
http:// _____
Email: _____

Website:
User Name: _____
PW: _____
http:// _____
Email: _____

Website:
User Name: _____
PW: _____
http:// _____
Email: _____

Website:
User Name: _____
PW: _____
http:// _____
Email: _____

Website:
User Name: _____
PW: _____
http:// _____
Email: _____

Website:
User Name: _____
PW: _____
http:// _____
Email: _____

Website:
User Name: _____
PW: _____
http:// _____
Email: _____

Website:
User Name: _____
PW: _____
http:// _____
Email: _____

Website:
User Name: _____
PW: _____
http:// _____
Email: _____

Website:
User Name: _____
PW: _____
http:// _____
Email: _____

Website:
User Name: _____
PW: _____
http:// _____
Email: _____

Website:
User Name: _____
PW: _____
http:// _____
Email: _____

Website:
User Name: _____
PW: _____
http:// _____
Email: _____

Website:
User Name: _____
PW: _____
http:// _____
Email: _____

Website:
User Name: _____
PW: _____
http:// _____
Email: _____

Website:
User Name: _____
PW: _____
http:// _____
Email: _____

Website:
User Name: _____
PW: _____
http:// _____
Email: _____

Website:
User Name: _____
PW: _____
http:// _____
Email: _____

Website:
User Name: _____
PW: _____
http:// _____
Email: _____

Website:
User Name: _____
PW: _____
http:// _____
Email: _____

Website:
User Name: _____
PW: _____
http:// _____
Email: _____

Website:
User Name: _____
PW: _____
http:// _____
Email: _____

Website:
User Name: _____
PW: _____
http:// _____
Email: _____

Website:
User Name: _____
PW: _____
http:// _____
Email: _____

Website:
User Name: _____
PW: _____
http:// _____
Email: _____

Website:
User Name: _____
PW: _____
http:// _____
Email: _____

Website:
User Name: _____
PW: _____
http:// _____
Email: _____

Website:
User Name: _____
PW: _____
http:// _____
Email: _____

Website:
User Name: _____
PW: _____
http:// _____
Email: _____

Website:
User Name: _____
PW: _____
http:// _____
Email: _____

Website:
User Name: _____
PW: _____
http:// _____
Email: _____

Website:
User Name: _____
PW: _____
http:// _____
Email: _____

Website:
User Name: _____
PW: _____
http:// _____
Email: _____

Website:
User Name: _____
PW: _____
http:// _____
Email: _____

Website:
User Name: _____
PW: _____
http:// _____
Email: _____

Website:
User Name: _____
PW: _____
http:// _____
Email: _____

Website:
User Name: _____
PW: _____
http:// _____
Email: _____

Website:
User Name: _____
PW: _____
http:// _____
Email: _____

Website:
User Name: _____
PW: _____
http:// _____
Email: _____

Website:
User Name: _____
PW: _____
http:// _____
Email: _____

Website:
User Name: _____
PW: _____
http:// _____
Email: _____

Website:
User Name: _____
PW: _____
http:// _____
Email: _____

Website:
User Name: _____
PW: _____
http:// _____
Email: _____

Website:
User Name: _____
PW: _____
http:// _____
Email: _____

Website:
User Name: _____
PW: _____
http:// _____
Email: _____

Website:
User Name: _____
PW: _____
http:// _____
Email: _____

Website:
User Name: _____
PW: _____
http:// _____
Email: _____

Website:
User Name: _____
PW: _____
http:// _____
Email: _____

Website:
User Name: _____
PW: _____
http:// _____
Email: _____

Website:
User Name: _____
PW: _____
http:// _____
Email: _____

Website:
User Name: _____
PW: _____
http:// _____
Email: _____

Website:
User Name: _____
PW: _____
http:// _____
Email: _____

Website:
User Name: _____
PW: _____
http:// _____
Email: _____

Website:
User Name: _____
PW: _____
http:// _____
Email: _____

Website:
User Name: _____
PW: _____
http:// _____
Email: _____

Website:
User Name: _____
PW: _____
http:// _____
Email: _____

Website:
User Name: _____
PW: _____
http:// _____
Email: _____

Website:
User Name: _____
PW: _____
http:// _____
Email: _____

Website:
User Name: _____
PW: _____
http:// _____
Email: _____

Website:
User Name: _____
PW: _____
http:// _____
Email: _____

Website:
User Name: _____
PW: _____
http:// _____
Email: _____

Website:
User Name: _____
PW: _____
http:// _____
Email: _____

Website:
User Name: _____
PW: _____
http:// _____
Email: _____

Website:
User Name: _____
PW: _____
http:// _____
Email: _____

Website:
User Name: _____
PW: _____
http:// _____
Email: _____

Website:
User Name: _____
PW: _____
http:// _____
Email: _____

Website:
User Name: _____
PW: _____
http:// _____
Email: _____

Website:
User Name: _____
PW: _____
http:// _____
Email: _____

Website:
User Name: _____
PW: _____
http:// _____
Email: _____

Website:
User Name: _____
PW: _____
http:// _____
Email: _____

Website:
User Name: _____
PW: _____
http:// _____
Email: _____

Website:
User Name: _____
PW: _____
http:// _____
Email: _____

Website:
User Name: _____
PW: _____
http:// _____
Email: _____

Website:
User Name: _____
PW: _____
http:// _____
Email: _____

Website:
User Name: _____
PW: _____
http:// _____
Email: _____

Website:
User Name: _____
PW: _____
http:// _____
Email: _____

Website:
User Name: _____
PW: _____
http:// _____
Email: _____

Website:
User Name: _____
PW: _____
http:// _____
Email: _____

Website:
User Name: _____
PW: _____
http:// _____
Email: _____

Website:
User Name: _____
PW: _____
http:// _____
Email: _____

Website:
User Name: _____
PW: _____
http:// _____
Email: _____

Website:
User Name: _____
PW: _____
http:// _____
Email: _____

Website:
User Name: _____
PW: _____
http:// _____
Email: _____

Website:
User Name: _____
PW: _____
http:// _____
Email: _____

Website:
User Name: _____
PW: _____
http:// _____
Email: _____

Website:
User Name: _____
PW: _____
http:// _____
Email: _____

Website:
User Name: _____
PW: _____
http:// _____
Email: _____

Website:
User Name: _____
PW: _____
http:// _____
Email: _____

Website:
User Name: _____
PW: _____
http:// _____
Email: _____

Website:
User Name: _____
PW: _____
http:// _____
Email: _____

Website:
User Name: _____
PW: _____
http:// _____
Email: _____

Website:
User Name: _____
PW: _____
http:// _____
Email: _____

Website:
User Name: _____
PW: _____
http:// _____
Email: _____

Website:
User Name: _____
PW: _____
http:// _____
Email: _____

Website:
User Name: _____
PW: _____
http:// _____
Email: _____

Website:
User Name: _____
PW: _____
http:// _____
Email: _____

Website:
User Name: _____
PW: _____
http:// _____
Email: _____

Website:
User Name: _____
PW: _____
http:// _____
Email: _____

Website:
User Name: _____
PW: _____
http:// _____
Email: _____

Website:
User Name: _____
PW: _____
http:// _____
Email: _____

Website:
User Name: _____
PW: _____
http:// _____
Email: _____

Website:
User Name: _____
PW: _____
http:// _____
Email: _____

Website:
User Name: _____
PW: _____
http:// _____
Email: _____

Website:
User Name: _____
PW: _____
http:// _____
Email: _____

Website:
User Name: _____
PW: _____
http:// _____
Email: _____

Website:
User Name: _____
PW: _____
http:// _____
Email: _____

Website:
User Name: _____
PW: _____
http:// _____
Email: _____

Website:
User Name: _____
PW: _____
http:// _____
Email: _____

Website:
User Name: _____
PW: _____
http:// _____
Email: _____

Website:
User Name: _____
PW: _____
http:// _____
Email: _____

Website:
User Name: _____
PW: _____
http:// _____
Email: _____

Website:
User Name: _____
PW: _____
http:// _____
Email: _____

Website:
User Name: _____
PW: _____
http:// _____
Email: _____

Website:
User Name: _____
PW: _____
http:// _____
Email: _____

Website:
User Name: _____
PW: _____
http:// _____
Email: _____

Website:
User Name: _____
PW: _____
http:// _____
Email: _____

Website:
User Name: _____
PW: _____
http:// _____
Email: _____

Website:
User Name: _____
PW: _____
http:// _____
Email: _____

Website:
User Name: _____
PW: _____
http:// _____
Email: _____

Website:
User Name: _____
PW: _____
http:// _____
Email: _____

Website:
User Name: _____
PW: _____
http:// _____
Email: _____

Website:
User Name: _____
PW: _____
http:// _____
Email: _____

Website:
User Name: _____
PW: _____
http:// _____
Email: _____

Website:
User Name: _____
PW: _____
http:// _____
Email: _____

Website:
User Name: _____
PW: _____
http:// _____
Email: _____

Website:
User Name: _____
PW: _____
http:// _____
Email: _____

Website:
User Name: _____
PW: _____
http:// _____
Email: _____

Website:
User Name: _____
PW: _____
http:// _____
Email: _____

Website:
User Name: _____
PW: _____
http:// _____
Email: _____

Website:
User Name: _____
PW: _____
http:// _____
Email: _____

Website:
User Name: _____
PW: _____
http:// _____
Email: _____

Website:
User Name: _____
PW: _____
http:// _____
Email: _____

Website:
User Name: _____
PW: _____
http:// _____
Email: _____

Website:
User Name: _____
PW: _____
http:// _____
Email: _____

Website:
User Name: _____
PW: _____
http:// _____
Email: _____

Website:
User Name: _____
PW: _____
http:// _____
Email: _____

Website:
User Name: _____
PW: _____
http:// _____
Email: _____

Website:
User Name: _____
PW: _____
http:// _____
Email: _____

Website:
User Name: _____
PW: _____
http:// _____
Email: _____

Website:
User Name: _____
PW: _____
http:// _____
Email: _____

Website:
User Name: _____
PW: _____
http:// _____
Email: _____

Website:
User Name: _____
PW: _____
http:// _____
Email: _____

Website:
User Name: _____
PW: _____
http:// _____
Email: _____

Website:
User Name: _____
PW: _____
http:// _____
Email: _____

Website:
User Name: _____
PW: _____
http:// _____
Email: _____

Website:
User Name: _____
PW: _____
http:// _____
Email: _____

Website:
User Name: _____
PW: _____
http:// _____
Email: _____

Website:
User Name: _____
PW: _____
http:// _____
Email: _____

Website:
User Name: _____
PW: _____
http:// _____
Email: _____

Website:
User Name: _____
PW: _____
http:// _____
Email: _____

Website:
User Name: _____
PW: _____
http:// _____
Email: _____

Website:
User Name: _____
PW: _____
http:// _____
Email: _____

Website:
User Name: _____
PW: _____
http:// _____
Email: _____

Website:
User Name: _____
PW: _____
http:// _____
Email: _____

Website:
User Name: _____
PW: _____
http:// _____
Email: _____

Website:
User Name: _____
PW: _____
http:// _____
Email: _____

Website:
User Name: _____
PW: _____
http:// _____
Email: _____

Website:
User Name: _____
PW: _____
http:// _____
Email: _____

Website:
User Name: _____
PW: _____
http:// _____
Email: _____

Website:
User Name: _____
PW: _____
http:// _____
Email: _____

Website:
User Name: _____
PW: _____
http:// _____
Email: _____

Website:
User Name: _____
PW: _____
http:// _____
Email: _____

Website:
User Name: _____
PW: _____
http:// _____
Email: _____

Website:
User Name: _____
PW: _____
http:// _____
Email: _____

Website:
User Name: _____
PW: _____
http:// _____
Email: _____

Website:
User Name: _____
PW: _____
http:// _____
Email: _____

Website:
User Name: _____
PW: _____
http:// _____
Email: _____

Website:
User Name: _____
PW: _____
http:// _____
Email: _____

Website:
User Name: _____
PW: _____
http:// _____
Email: _____

Website:
User Name: _____
PW: _____
http:// _____
Email: _____

Website:
User Name: _____
PW: _____
http:// _____
Email: _____

Website:
User Name: _____
PW: _____
http:// _____
Email: _____

Website:
User Name: _____
PW: _____
http:// _____
Email: _____

Website:
User Name: _____
PW: _____
http:// _____
Email: _____

Website:
User Name: _____
PW: _____
http:// _____
Email: _____

Website:
User Name: _____
PW: _____
http:// _____
Email: _____

Website:
User Name: _____
PW: _____
http:// _____
Email: _____

Website:
User Name: _____
PW: _____
http:// _____
Email: _____

Website:
User Name: _____
PW: _____
http:// _____
Email: _____

Website:
User Name: _____
PW: _____
http:// _____
Email: _____

Website:
User Name: _____
PW: _____
http:// _____
Email: _____

Website:
User Name: _____
PW: _____
http:// _____
Email: _____

Website:
User Name: _____
PW: _____
http:// _____
Email: _____

Website:
User Name: _____
PW: _____
http:// _____
Email: _____

Website:
User Name: _____
PW: _____
http:// _____
Email: _____

Website:
User Name: _____

PW: _____

http:// _____

Email: _____

Website:
User Name: _____

PW: _____

http:// _____

Email: _____

Website:
User Name: _____

PW: _____

http:// _____

Email: _____

Website:
User Name: _____

PW: _____

http:// _____

Email: _____

Website:
User Name: _____

PW: _____

http:// _____

Email: _____

Website:
User Name: _____
PW: _____
http:// _____
Email: _____

Website:
User Name: _____
PW: _____
http:// _____
Email: _____

Website:
User Name: _____
PW: _____
http:// _____
Email: _____

Website:
User Name: _____
PW: _____
http:// _____
Email: _____

Website:
User Name: _____
PW: _____
http:// _____
Email: _____

Website:
User Name: _____
PW: _____
http:// _____
Email: _____

Website:
User Name: _____
PW: _____
http:// _____
Email: _____

Website:
User Name: _____
PW: _____
http:// _____
Email: _____

Website:
User Name: _____
PW: _____
http:// _____
Email: _____

Website:
User Name: _____
PW: _____
http:// _____
Email: _____

Website:
User Name: _____
PW: _____
http:// _____
Email: _____

Website:
User Name: _____
PW: _____
http:// _____
Email: _____

Website:
User Name: _____
PW: _____
http:// _____
Email: _____

Website:
User Name: _____
PW: _____
http:// _____
Email: _____

Website:
User Name: _____
PW: _____
http:// _____
Email: _____

Website:
User Name: _____
PW: _____
http:// _____
Email: _____

Website:
User Name: _____
PW: _____
http:// _____
Email: _____

Website:
User Name: _____
PW: _____
http:// _____
Email: _____

Website:
User Name: _____
PW: _____
http:// _____
Email: _____

Website:
User Name: _____
PW: _____
http:// _____
Email: _____

Website:
User Name: _____
PW: _____
http:// _____
Email: _____

Website:
User Name: _____
PW: _____
http:// _____
Email: _____

Website:
User Name: _____
PW: _____
http:// _____
Email: _____

Website:
User Name: _____
PW: _____
http:// _____
Email: _____

Website:
User Name: _____
PW: _____
http:// _____
Email: _____

Website:
User Name: _____
PW: _____
http:// _____
Email: _____

Website:
User Name: _____
PW: _____
http:// _____
Email: _____

Website:
User Name: _____
PW: _____
http:// _____
Email: _____

Website:
User Name: _____
PW: _____
http:// _____
Email: _____

Website:
User Name: _____
PW: _____
http:// _____
Email: _____

Website:
User Name: _____
PW: _____
http:// _____
Email: _____

Website:
User Name: _____
PW: _____
http:// _____
Email: _____

Website:
User Name: _____
PW: _____
http:// _____
Email: _____

Website:
User Name: _____
PW: _____
http:// _____
Email: _____

Website:
User Name: _____
PW: _____
http:// _____
Email: _____

Website:
User Name: _____
PW: _____
http:// _____
Email: _____

Website:
User Name: _____
PW: _____
http:// _____
Email: _____

Website:
User Name: _____
PW: _____
http:// _____
Email: _____

Website:
User Name: _____
PW: _____
http:// _____
Email: _____

Website:
User Name: _____
PW: _____
http:// _____
Email: _____

Website:
User Name: _____
PW: _____
http:// _____
Email: _____

Website:
User Name: _____
PW: _____
http:// _____
Email: _____

Website:
User Name: _____
PW: _____
http:// _____
Email: _____

Website:
User Name: _____
PW: _____
http:// _____
Email: _____

Website:
User Name: _____
PW: _____
http:// _____
Email: _____

Website:
User Name: _____
PW: _____
http:// _____
Email: _____

Website:
User Name: _____
PW: _____
http:// _____
Email: _____

Website:
User Name: _____
PW: _____
http:// _____
Email: _____

Website:
User Name: _____
PW: _____
http:// _____
Email: _____

Website:
User Name: _____
PW: _____
http:// _____
Email: _____

Website:
User Name: _____
PW: _____
http:// _____
Email: _____

Website:
User Name: _____
PW: _____
http:// _____
Email: _____

Website:
User Name: _____
PW: _____
http:// _____
Email: _____

Website:
User Name: _____
PW: _____
http:// _____
Email: _____

Website:
User Name: _____
PW: _____
http:// _____
Email: _____

Website:
User Name: _____
PW: _____
http:// _____
Email: _____

Website:
User Name: _____
PW: _____
http:// _____
Email: _____

Website:
User Name: _____
PW: _____
http:// _____
Email: _____

Website:
User Name: _____
PW: _____
http:// _____
Email: _____

Website:
User Name: _____
PW: _____
http:// _____
Email: _____

Website:
User Name: _____
PW: _____
http:// _____
Email: _____

Website:
User Name: _____
PW: _____
http:// _____
Email: _____

Website:
User Name: _____
PW: _____
http:// _____
Email: _____

Website:
User Name: _____
PW: _____
http:// _____
Email: _____

Website:
User Name: _____
PW: _____
http:// _____
Email: _____

Website:
User Name: _____
PW: _____
http:// _____
Email: _____

Website:
User Name: _____
PW: _____
http:// _____
Email: _____

Website:
User Name: _____
PW: _____
http:// _____
Email: _____

Website:
User Name: _____
PW: _____
http:// _____
Email: _____

Website:
User Name: _____
PW: _____
http:// _____
Email: _____

Website:
User Name: _____
PW: _____
http:// _____
Email: _____

Website:
User Name: _____
PW: _____
http:// _____
Email: _____

Website:
User Name: _____
PW: _____
http:// _____
Email: _____

Website:
User Name: _____
PW: _____
http:// _____
Email: _____

Website:
User Name: _____
PW: _____
http:// _____
Email: _____

Website:
User Name: _____
PW: _____
http:// _____
Email: _____

Website:
User Name: _____
PW: _____
http:// _____
Email: _____

Website:
User Name: _____
PW: _____
http:// _____
Email: _____

Website:
User Name: _____
PW: _____
http:// _____
Email: _____

Website:
User Name: _____
PW: _____
http:// _____
Email: _____

Website:
User Name: _____
PW: _____
http:// _____
Email: _____

Website:
User Name: _____
PW: _____
http:// _____
Email: _____

Website:
User Name: _____
PW: _____
http:// _____
Email: _____

Website:
User Name: _____
PW: _____
http:// _____
Email: _____

Website:
User Name: _____
PW: _____
http:// _____
Email: _____

Website:
User Name: _____
PW: _____
http:// _____
Email: _____

Website:
User Name: _____
PW: _____
http:// _____
Email: _____

Website:
User Name: _____
PW: _____
http:// _____
Email: _____

Website:
User Name: _____
PW: _____
http:// _____
Email: _____

Website:
User Name: _____
PW: _____
http:// _____
Email: _____

Website:
User Name: _____
PW: _____
http:// _____
Email: _____

Website:
User Name: _____
PW: _____
http:// _____
Email: _____

Website:
User Name: _____
PW: _____
http:// _____
Email: _____

Website:
User Name: _____
PW: _____
http:// _____
Email: _____

Website:
User Name: _____
PW: _____
http:// _____
Email: _____

Website:
User Name: _____
PW: _____
http:// _____
Email: _____

Website:
User Name: _____
PW: _____
http:// _____
Email: _____

Website:
User Name: _____
PW: _____
http:// _____
Email: _____

Website:
User Name: _____
PW: _____
http:// _____
Email: _____

Website:
User Name: _____
PW: _____
http:// _____
Email: _____

Website:
User Name: _____
PW: _____
http:// _____
Email: _____

Website:
User Name: _____
PW: _____
http:// _____
Email: _____

Website:
User Name: _____
PW: _____
http:// _____
Email: _____

Website:
User Name: _____
PW: _____
http:// _____
Email: _____

Website:
User Name: _____
PW: _____
http:// _____
Email: _____

Website:
User Name: _____
PW: _____
http:// _____
Email: _____

Website:
User Name: _____
PW: _____
http:// _____
Email: _____

Website:
User Name: _____
PW: _____
http:// _____
Email: _____

Website:
User Name: _____
PW: _____
http:// _____
Email: _____

Website:
User Name: _____
PW: _____
http:// _____
Email: _____

Website:
User Name: _____
PW: _____
http:// _____
Email: _____

Website:
User Name: _____
PW: _____
http:// _____
Email: _____

Website:
User Name: _____
PW: _____
http:// _____
Email: _____

Website:
User Name: _____
PW: _____
http:// _____
Email: _____

Website:
User Name: _____
PW: _____
http:// _____
Email: _____

Website:
User Name: _____
PW: _____
http:// _____
Email: _____

Website:
User Name: _____
PW: _____
http:// _____
Email: _____

Website:
User Name: _____
PW: _____
http:// _____
Email: _____

Website:
User Name: _____
PW: _____
http:// _____
Email: _____

Website:
User Name: _____
PW: _____
http:// _____
Email: _____

Website:
User Name: _____
PW: _____
http:// _____
Email: _____

Website:
User Name: _____
PW: _____
http:// _____
Email: _____

Website:
User Name: _____
PW: _____
http:// _____
Email: _____

Website:
User Name: _____
PW: _____
http:// _____
Email: _____

Website:
User Name: _____
PW: _____
http:// _____
Email: _____

Website:
User Name: _____
PW: _____
http:// _____
Email: _____

Website:
User Name: _____
PW: _____
http:// _____
Email: _____

Website:
User Name: _____
PW: _____
http:// _____
Email: _____

Website:
User Name: _____
PW: _____
http:// _____
Email: _____

Website:
User Name: _____
PW: _____
http:// _____
Email: _____

Website:
User Name: _____
PW: _____
http:// _____
Email: _____

Website:
User Name: _____
PW: _____
http:// _____
Email: _____

Website:
User Name: _____
PW: _____
http:// _____
Email: _____

Website:
User Name: _____
PW: _____
http:// _____
Email: _____

Website:
User Name: _____
PW: _____
http:// _____
Email: _____

Website:
User Name: _____
PW: _____
http:// _____
Email: _____

Website:
User Name: _____
PW: _____
http:// _____
Email: _____

Website:
User Name: _____
PW: _____
http:// _____
Email: _____

Website:
User Name: _____
PW: _____
http:// _____
Email: _____

Website:
User Name: _____
PW: _____
http:// _____
Email: _____

Website:
User Name: _____
PW: _____
http:// _____
Email: _____

Website:
User Name: _____
PW: _____
http:// _____
Email: _____

Website:
User Name: _____
PW: _____
http:// _____
Email: _____

Website:
User Name: _____
PW: _____
http:// _____
Email: _____

Website:
User Name: _____
PW: _____
http:// _____
Email: _____

Website:
User Name: _____
PW: _____
http:// _____
Email: _____

Website:
User Name: _____
PW: _____
http:// _____
Email: _____

Website:
User Name: _____
PW: _____
http:// _____
Email: _____

Website:
User Name: _____
PW: _____
http:// _____
Email: _____

Website:
User Name: _____
PW: _____
http:// _____
Email: _____

Website:
User Name: _____
PW: _____
http:// _____
Email: _____

Website:
User Name: _____
PW: _____
http:// _____
Email: _____

Website:
User Name: _____
PW: _____
http:// _____
Email: _____

Website:
User Name: _____
PW: _____
http:// _____
Email: _____

Website:
User Name: _____
PW: _____
http:// _____
Email: _____

Website:
User Name: _____
PW: _____
http:// _____
Email: _____

Website:
User Name: _____
PW: _____
http:// _____
Email: _____

Website:
User Name: _____
PW: _____
http:// _____
Email: _____

Website:
User Name: _____
PW: _____
http:// _____
Email: _____

Website:
User Name: _____
PW: _____
http:// _____
Email: _____

Website:
User Name: _____
PW: _____
http:// _____
Email: _____

Website:
User Name: _____
PW: _____
http:// _____
Email: _____

Website:
User Name: _____
PW: _____
http:// _____
Email: _____

Website:
User Name: _____
PW: _____
http:// _____
Email: _____

Website:
User Name: _____
PW: _____
http:// _____
Email: _____

Website:

User Name: _____

PW: _____

http:// _____

Email: _____

Website:

User Name: _____

PW: _____

http:// _____

Email: _____

Website:

User Name: _____

PW: _____

http:// _____

Email: _____

Website:

User Name: _____

PW: _____

http:// _____

Email: _____

Website:

User Name: _____

PW: _____

http:// _____

Email: _____

Website:
User Name: _____
PW: _____
http:// _____
Email: _____

Website:
User Name: _____
PW: _____
http:// _____
Email: _____

Website:
User Name: _____
PW: _____
http:// _____
Email: _____

Website:
User Name: _____
PW: _____
http:// _____
Email: _____

Website:
User Name: _____
PW: _____
http:// _____
Email: _____

Website:
User Name: _____
PW: _____
http:// _____
Email: _____

Website:
User Name: _____
PW: _____
http:// _____
Email: _____

Website:
User Name: _____
PW: _____
http:// _____
Email: _____

Website:
User Name: _____
PW: _____
http:// _____
Email: _____

Website:
User Name: _____
PW: _____
http:// _____
Email: _____

Website:
User Name: _____
PW: _____
http:// _____
Email: _____

Website:
User Name: _____
PW: _____
http:// _____
Email: _____

Website:
User Name: _____
PW: _____
http:// _____
Email: _____

Website:
User Name: _____
PW: _____
http:// _____
Email: _____

Website:
User Name: _____
PW: _____
http:// _____
Email: _____

Website:
User Name: _____
PW: _____
http:// _____
Email: _____

Website:
User Name: _____
PW: _____
http:// _____
Email: _____

Website:
User Name: _____
PW: _____
http:// _____
Email: _____

Website:
User Name: _____
PW: _____
http:// _____
Email: _____

Website:
User Name: _____
PW: _____
http:// _____
Email: _____

Website:
User Name: _____
PW: _____
http:// _____
Email: _____

Website:
User Name: _____
PW: _____
http:// _____
Email: _____

Website:
User Name: _____
PW: _____
http:// _____
Email: _____

Website:
User Name: _____
PW: _____
http:// _____
Email: _____

Website:
User Name: _____
PW: _____
http:// _____
Email: _____

Website:
User Name: _____
PW: _____
http:// _____
Email: _____

Website:
User Name: _____
PW: _____
http:// _____
Email: _____

Website:
User Name: _____
PW: _____
http:// _____
Email: _____

Website:
User Name: _____
PW: _____
http:// _____
Email: _____

Website:
User Name: _____
PW: _____
http:// _____
Email: _____

Website:
User Name: _____
PW: _____
http:// _____
Email: _____

Website:
User Name: _____
PW: _____
http:// _____
Email: _____

Website:
User Name: _____
PW: _____
http:// _____
Email: _____

Website:
User Name: _____
PW: _____
http:// _____
Email: _____

Website:
User Name: _____
PW: _____
http:// _____
Email: _____

Website:
User Name: _____
PW: _____
http:// _____
Email: _____

Website:
User Name: _____
PW: _____
http:// _____
Email: _____

Website:
User Name: _____
PW: _____
http:// _____
Email: _____

Website:
User Name: _____
PW: _____
http:// _____
Email: _____

Website:
User Name: _____
PW: _____
http:// _____
Email: _____

Website:
User Name: _____
PW: _____
http:// _____
Email: _____

Website:
User Name: _____
PW: _____
http:// _____
Email: _____

Website:
User Name: _____
PW: _____
http:// _____
Email: _____

Website:
User Name: _____
PW: _____
http:// _____
Email: _____

Website:
User Name: _____
PW: _____
http:// _____
Email: _____

Website:
User Name: _____
PW: _____
http:// _____
Email: _____

Website:
User Name: _____
PW: _____
http:// _____
Email: _____

Website:
User Name: _____
PW: _____
http:// _____
Email: _____

Website:
User Name: _____
PW: _____
http:// _____
Email: _____

Website:
User Name: _____
PW: _____
http:// _____
Email: _____

Website:
User Name: _____
PW: _____
http:// _____
Email: _____

Website:
User Name: _____
PW: _____
http:// _____
Email: _____

Website:
User Name: _____
PW: _____
http:// _____
Email: _____

Website:
User Name: _____
PW: _____
http:// _____
Email: _____

Website:
User Name: _____
PW: _____
http:// _____
Email: _____

Website:
User Name: _____
PW: _____
http:// _____
Email: _____

Website:
User Name: _____
PW: _____
http:// _____
Email: _____

Website:
User Name: _____
PW: _____
http:// _____
Email: _____

Website:
User Name: _____
PW: _____
http:// _____
Email: _____

Website:
User Name: _____
PW: _____
http:// _____
Email: _____

Website:
User Name: _____
PW: _____
http:// _____
Email: _____

Website:
User Name: _____
PW: _____
http:// _____
Email: _____

Website:
User Name: _____
PW: _____
http:// _____
Email: _____

Website:
User Name: _____
PW: _____
http:// _____
Email: _____

Website:
User Name: _____
PW: _____
http:// _____
Email: _____

Website:
User Name: _____
PW: _____
http:// _____
Email: _____

Website:
User Name: _____
PW: _____
http:// _____
Email: _____

Website:
User Name: _____
PW: _____
http:// _____
Email: _____

Website:
User Name: _____
PW: _____
http:// _____
Email: _____

Website:
User Name: _____
PW: _____
http:// _____
Email: _____

Frequently Called Numbers

Website:
User Name: _____
PW: _____
http:// _____
Email: _____

Website:
User Name: _____
PW: _____
http:// ___ _____
Email: _____

Website:
User Name: _____
PW: _____
http:// _____
Email: _____

Website:
User Name: _____
PW: _____
http:// _____
Email: _____

Website:
User Name: _____
PW: _____
http://_____ _____
Email: _____

Website:
User Name: _____
PW: _____
http:// _____
Email: _____

Website:
User Name: _____
PW: _____
http:// ___ _____
Email: _____

Website:
User Name: _____
PW: _____
http:// _____
Email: _____

Website:
User Name: _____
PW: _____
http:// _____
Email: _____

Website:
User Name: _____
PW: _____
http:// _____
Email: _____

Class Schedule

Day	Period	Class	Instructor	Test Due

THINGS TO DO

THINGS TO DO

Help For Seniors

Some Resources to guide you:

- The Eldercare Locator identifies state and area agencies on aging that can refer you to local services. Call (800) 677-1116 between 8 a.m. and 9 p.m. weekdays. Eastern Standard Time (EST) is prepared with the zip code of the person to be helped.

  www.elderaffairs.state.fl.us/   English/cares.html

- The **U.S. Administration on Aging** Web Site at www.aoa.gov offers details on local resources, and links to other useful Web sites.

- **The AARP Web site**, www.aarp.org/caregive, details types of help available. Post questions and comments at the Caregivers Circle at www.aarp.org/healthguide or join the online support group at ADL at 8:30 p.m. EST on Wednesdays (keyword: AARP) " A caregiver guide to information and Resources." (D16697) is available from AARP **Fulfillment EEO** -1371, 601 E St NW, Washington, D.C. 20049

- **Medic-Alert**
  http://www.alert-1.com/

- **The visiting Nurse Association of America** can identify local visiting nurse agencies that operate in 40 states. Check the Web Site at www. Vnaa.org or call 1-800-866-8773 toll free.

- **The National Association of professional Geriatric Care** Managers sells each consumer directory for $15. Call (520-881-8008) Web address: www.caremanager.org

- **The National Family Caregivers Association** at (800)896-3650 offers support and info Web site: www.nfcacares.org

- **The National Assoc. of Home Care Provider**: at www.nahc.org or call (202)547-7424. They offer a Consumer Guide "How to choose a Home-Care Provider" or write to 228 7th St S.E.,

Hot Links

For Broadband and Hi Speed Internet Access

Adelphia: $23.95 per month faster than DSL

Brighthouse: Check website for fees

Bell South: Has DSL

Charter: $14.95 per 6 month– increases after that 5mps speeds

Comcast: Hi-speed access $19.959 per 6 month

Cox.com/net $19.95 for 1st 3 month changes after that

EarthLink: As low as $12.95 per mos. Hi speed internet access and more

insighthighspeed: $30.00 per month per year

Media.com: $19.95 for 1 year 5 xs faster than DSL

Net Zero: $6.95—$14.95 2GB   10GB Free email storage and more

Optimum: $29.95 per month 1 year—5x faster than DSL

PeoplePc: $10.95 a month with 12 month commitment and

Road Runner: $29.95 per month—*Fast* hi speed internet

Verizon.net/com: Has DSl, Dish Network and Fios - Check site for fees

Birthdays

Anniversaries

Dates

IMPORTANT EVENTS

JANUARY	JULY
FEBRUARY	AUGUST
MARCH	SEPTEMBER
APRIL	OCTOBER
MAY	NOVEMBER
JUNE	DECEMBER

Troubleshooting Hints for Dummies

Some Helpful Tips

It's a dreadful way to start a day - you press the power button on your computer and nothing happens. Do not fear because all may not be lost! Follow these simple steps to determine why your computer won't turn on.

Note: It is very important to troubleshoot any issue beginning with the most likely and easily testable problem so be sure to follow these steps in order.

As silly as it may sound, the number one reason why a computer won't turn on is because it wasn't turned on! Before starting a sometimes time consuming troubleshooting process, make sure you've turned on every **power switch and power button** associated with your computer: **_Definition_**: The power button is a usually round or square button that powers on and powers off a device. Typically, the device powers on; when the switch is pressed in and powers off when the button is again pressed. Some devices instead have a power switch that accomplishes the same thing. A flip of the switch in one direction turns the device on and a flip in the other turns the device off.

Nearly all electronic devices have power buttons or power switches. In a typical computer setup, power buttons and switches appear on the front and sometimes back of the monitor and on the front and back of the case. The power switch on the back of the case is actually the power switch for the power supply installed in the computer.

Power buttons and switches are usually labeled with "I" and "O" symbols. The "I" represents *power on* and the "O" represents *power off*. This designation will sometimes be seen as I/O or as the "I" and "O" characters on top of each other as a single character.

Also Known As: power switch

Power button switch is on the front of the computer's case.
Power button switch is on the front and/or back of the monitor.
Power switch on the power supply is on the back of the computer.
Power switch on the power strip or surge protector (if you have one).

Verify that the power supply voltage switch is correctly set. If the input voltage for the power supply does not match the correct setting for your country, your computer may not power on.

Check for loose computer and monitor power cable connections. A loose or unplugged power cable is one of the top reasons why a computer doesn't turn on.

- **Perform a "lamp test" to verify power is being provided.** Your computer isn't going to turn on if it's not getting power so you need to make sure that the power source is working properly

- Do a quick test of the power supply by holding your hand behind the power supply fan located at the rear of the case. If the power supply is working, you should feel air from within the case blowing against your hand. If not, you may need to replace the power supply.

Tip: Is the power light on the front of the computer's case on? If you've turned the power switch on but the light is off, this is

another good indication that the power supply is the cause of this issue.

Over time, internal components and the cables that connect them can wiggle loose which often times can result in a computer unable to power on. Try resetting the following and then try to power on the computer again:

Reseat the internal cables

Reseat the memory modules

Reseat the video card

Reseat other expansion cards

Reseating the CPU may also be necessary but should only be attempted if the reseating of all other components is not successful. This is due to the fact that this process is a little more involved and can run a small risk of damage to the **CPU**. This isn't a big concern if you're careful, so don't worry!

Check for causes of electrical shorts in the computer case. This is often the cause of the problem when the computer powers on for a second or two but then powers off completely

Most monitors have a small light next to the power button that can change between various colors. If the screen is blank, this light is your main source of information about the monitor.

If this light is not on at all, double-check the power switch and connections (Steps 1, 2 and 3) and also make sure the monitor cable is securely plugged in to the **video card** port on the back of the computer case. If the light is still off, replace the monitor. If it comes back on, try starting your computer again - a loose or unplugged monitor cable may have been the issue all along.

What is a Video Card? The video card is an expansion card that allows the computer to send graphical information to a video display device such as a **monitor** or projector.

What is a Monitor? The monitor displays the video and graphics information generated by the computer through the **video card.** Monitors are very similar to televisions but display information at a

106

much higher quality.

- **An amber or yellow power light** simply means that the monitor is not receiving any information from the computer. In and of itself, this doesn't tell us much.

- **On the other hand, if the light is amber or yellow, the computer power light is on,** and the <u>hard drive</u> is active (making familiar sounds and the <u>hard drive activity light</u> on the computer case is blinking), the computer is probably starting normally but the video card is not   sending information to the monitor. ***Replace the video card.***

Beep codes (see Step 11) usually sound when a video card has malfunctioned but this is not always the case.

- **Is your computer making a beeping sound? Sometimes a computer will turn on just enough to play a series of beeps from the speakers.**

- **These *beep codes* play in particular sequences and represent a specific problem that your computer is having. <u>Troubleshoot the beep code</u> to figure out what its saying <u>and</u> then service the computer as necessary. Best to get a technician to take care of this for you. Unless you know what you are doing.**

Tips:

1. **Still can't get your computer to turn on? Let a community of computer support enthusiasts help out! Post the details of your problem in the <u>Focus on PC Support Forums</u>. Such as http://pcsupport.about.com/mpboards.htm**

Protect your Computer

Protecting your computer from viruses etc should not be a time consuming chore. But picking and installing the right software is the most important thing to start with.

I have found that installing Firefox/Mozilla has some great precautionary measures for surfing the web. With Firefox you can stop pop-ups or control them,

Windows Defender is also another excellent safe guard for your computer as well as AVG; both by the way are free but very effective.

CCleaner is great for clearing out those nuisance cookies and temp files that slow down your computer, also free.

BE CAREFULL WHAT YOU DOWNLOAD INTO YOUR COMPUTER; FROM THE INTERNET; MAKE SURE IT COMES FROM A TRUSTED SOURCE OR YOU WILL HAVE A BIG HEADACHE CLEANING IT UP IF YOU GET AN UNKNOWN VIRUS.

It is important that you update your important Program Files in order to make sure you are fully protected.

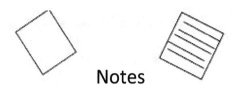

Notes

Free Medical Clinics /Camps All Over USA

Get the most recent information on Free Medical Clinics and Free Dental Clinics

http://www.freemedicalcamps.com/

Alabama

Alaska

Arizona

Arkansas

California

Colorado

Connecticut

Delaware

Florida

Georgia

Hawaii

Idaho

Illinois

Iowa

Kansas

Kentucky

Louisiana

Maine

Maryland

Massachusetts

Michigan

Minnesota

Mississippi

Missouri

Montana

Nebraska

Nevada

New Hampshire

New Jersey

New Mexico

New York

North Carolina

North Dakota

Ohio

Oklahoma

Oregon

Pennsylvania

Rhode Island

South Carolina

South Dakota

Tennessee

Texas

Utah

Vermont

Virginia

Washington

West Virginia

Wisconsin

Wyoming

Free Medical Clinics Cont....

American Samoa
District of Columbia
Federated States of
Micronesia
Guam

Virgin Islands
Marshall Islands
Northern Mariana Islands
Palau
Puerto Rico

Newly Added Sites

Bradley Free Clinic
Port Ministries
Light of the World Clinic / Clinical Luz Del Mundo
Reach Out for Kids Pediatric Clinic
Reach Out of Montgomery County Medical Clinic
Community Clinic of Rutherford County
Bothell Community Health Center
Institute for Behavior Change
The Floating Hospital
ABBA, A Women's Resource Center

2009

January
Su	Mo	Tu	We	Th	Fr	Sa
				1	2	3
4	5	6	7	8	9	10
11	12	13	14	15	16	17
18	19	20	21	22	23	24
25	26	27	28	29	30	31

February
Su	Mo	Tu	We	Th	Fr	Sa
1	2	3	4	5	6	7
8	9	10	11	12	13	14
15	16	17	18	19	20	21
22	23	24	25	26	27	28

March
Su	Mo	Tu	We	Th	Fr	Sa
1	2	3	4	5	6	7
8	9	10	11	12	13	14
15	16	17	18	19	20	21
22	23	24	25	26	27	28
29	30	31				

April
Su	Mo	Tu	We	Th	Fr	Sa
			1	2	3	4
5	6	7	8	9	10	11
12	13	14	15	16	17	18
19	20	21	22	23	24	25
26	27	28	29	30		

May
Su	Mo	Tu	We	Th	Fr	Sa
					1	2
3	4	5	6	7	8	9
10	11	12	13	14	15	16
17	18	19	20	21	22	23
24	25	26	27	28	29	30
31						

June
Su	Mo	Tu	We	Th	Fr	Sa
	1	2	3	4	5	6
7	8	9	10	11	12	13
14	15	16	17	18	19	20
21	22	23	24	25	26	27
28	29	30				

July
Su	Mo	Tu	We	Th	Fr	Sa
			1	2	3	4
5	6	7	8	9	10	11
12	13	14	15	16	17	18
19	20	21	22	23	24	25
26	27	28	29	30	31	

August
Su	Mo	Tu	We	Th	Fr	Sa
						1
2	3	4	5	6	7	8
9	10	11	12	13	14	15
16	17	18	19	20	21	22
23	24	25	26	27	28	29
30	31					

September
Su	Mo	Tu	We	Th	Fr	Sa
		1	2	3	4	5
6	7	8	9	10	11	12
13	14	15	16	17	18	19
20	21	22	23	24	25	26
27	28	29	30			

October
Su	Mo	Tu	We	Th	Fr	Sa
				1	2	3
4	5	6	7	8	9	10
11	12	13	14	15	16	17
18	19	20	21	22	23	24
25	26	27	28	29	30	31

November
Su	Mo	Tu	We	Th	Fr	Sa
1	2	3	4	5	6	7
8	9	10	11	12	13	14
15	16	17	18	19	20	21
22	23	24	25	26	27	28
29	30					

December
Su	Mo	Tu	We	Th	Fr	Sa
		1	2	3	4	5
6	7	8	9	10	11	12
13	14	15	16	17	18	19
20	21	22	23	24	25	26
27	28	29	30	31		

2010

January
Su	Mo	Tu	We	Th	Fr	Sa
					1	2
3	4	5	6	7	8	9
10	11	12	13	14	15	16
17	18	19	20	21	22	23
24	25	26	27	28	29	30
31						

February
Su	Mo	Tu	We	Th	Fr	Sa
	1	2	3	4	5	6
7	8	9	10	11	12	13
14	15	16	17	18	19	20
21	22	23	24	25	26	27
28						

March
Su	Mo	Tu	We	Th	Fr	Sa
	1	2	3	4	5	6
7	8	9	10	11	12	13
14	15	16	17	18	19	20
21	22	23	24	25	26	27
28	29	30	31			

April
Su	Mo	Tu	We	Th	Fr	Sa
				1	2	3
4	5	6	7	8	9	10
11	12	13	14	15	16	17
18	19	20	21	22	23	24
25	26	27	28	29	30	

May
Su	Mo	Tu	We	Th	Fr	Sa
						1
2	3	4	5	6	7	8
9	10	11	12	13	14	15
16	17	18	19	20	21	22
23	24	25	26	27	28	29
30	31					

June
Su	Mo	Tu	We	Th	Fr	Sa
		1	2	3	4	5
6	7	8	9	10	11	12
13	14	15	16	17	18	19
20	21	22	23	24	25	26
27	28	29	30			

July
Su	Mo	Tu	We	Th	Fr	Sa
				1	2	3
4	5	6	7	8	9	10
11	12	13	14	15	16	17
18	19	20	21	22	23	24
25	26	27	28	29	30	31

August
Su	Mo	Tu	We	Th	Fr	Sa
1	2	3	4	5	6	7
8	9	10	11	12	13	14
15	16	17	18	19	20	21
22	23	24	25	26	27	28
29	30	31				

September
Su	Mo	Tu	We	Th	Fr	Sa
			1	2	3	4
5	6	7	8	9	10	11
12	13	14	15	16	17	18
19	20	21	22	23	24	25
26	27	28	29	30		

October
Su	Mo	Tu	We	Th	Fr	Sa
					1	2
3	4	5	6	7	8	9
10	11	12	13	14	15	16
17	18	19	20	21	22	23
24	25	26	27	28	29	30
31						

November
Su	Mo	Tu	We	Th	Fr	Sa
	1	2	3	4	5	6
7	8	9	10	11	12	13
14	15	16	17	18	19	20
21	22	23	24	25	26	27
28	29	30				

December
Su	Mo	Tu	We	Th	Fr	Sa
			1	2	3	4
5	6	7	8	9	10	11
12	13	14	15	16	17	18
19	20	21	22	23	24	25
26	27	28	29	30	31	

HOLIDAYS AND OBSERVANCES

Since I do not know all the Holidays around the World I Need Your Help! Feel Free To Add Your To The Book And Sent Me An Update Of The Holiday So It Can Be Entered In Our 2009's

Jan 1 New Year's Day	Feb 18 Washington's Birthday	Mar 23 Easter Sunday
Jan 10 First of Muharram	Feb.24 Flag Day President's Day	April 20 1st Day of Passover
Jan. 19 Ashura	March 10 Eastern Orthodox Lent begins	May 1 Holocaust Remembrance Day
Feb 6 Ash Wednesday	March 16 Palm Sunday	May 5 Battle of Puebla
Feb 7 Lunar Day	Mar. 17 St. Patrick's Day	May 17 Armed Forces Day
Feb. 12 Lincoln's Birthday	March 20 Spring Begins	May 26 Memorial Day
Feb 14 Valentine's Day	March 21 Good Friday	June 14 Flag Day
Feb 21 Martin Luther King	March 21 Benito Juarez Birthday	June 15 Father's Day
Mar 16 Palm Sunday	Mar 21 Purim	May 11 Mother's Day

Jun 21 St John Baptiste Day (Quebec)	Oct.2 (Eid) alfitr	Nov. 20 Revolution Anniversary
July 1 Canada Day	Oct 13 Columbus Day	Nov 27 Thanksgiving Day
July 4th Independence Day	Oct 14 1st Day of Succoth	Dec. 7th Pearl Harbor Day
August 4 Civic Holiday	Oct. 24 United Nations Day	Dec. 21 Winter Begins
Sept. 1st First of Ramadan	Oct 31 Halloween	Dec 22 1st Day of Hanukah
Sept 1 Labor Day	Nov. 1st All Saints Day	Dec 25 Christmas Day
Sept. 2 Patriot Day	Nov. 2nd Day of the Dead	Nov 27 Thanksgiving Day
Sept. 11 Declaration of Independence Day	Nov. 4 Election Day	
Sept. 22 Autumn Begins	Nov 11 Veterans Day	
Sept 30 Rosh Hashanah	Nov. 11 Remembrance Day	

Weights & Measures

WEIGHT		VOLUME	
lb - Kg	Kg. - Lb	Gal. - L.	L. - Gal.
1 - 0.45	1 - 2.21	1. - 3.79	1 - 0.26
2 - 0.91	\2 - 4.41	2 - 7.57	2 - 0.53
3 - 1.36	3\- 6.61	3 - 11.35	3 - 0.79
4 - 1.81	4 - 15.14	4 - 15.14	4 - 1.06
5 - 2.27	5 - 11.32	5 - 18.93	5 - 1.32
6 - 2.72	6 - 13.23	6 - 22.71	6 - 1.59
7 - 3.18	7 - 15.43	7 - 26.50	7 - 1.85
8 - 3.63	8 - 17.64	8 - 30.28	8 - 2.11
9 - 4.08	9 - 19.84	9 - 34.16	9 - 2.38
10 - 4.54	10 - 22.05	10 -37.94	10 - 2.64
50 - 22.68	50 - 110.23	50 - 189.70	50 - 13.20
100-45.36	100 - 220.46	100-379.40	100 - 26.40

LENGTH

In. - M.	Cm. - In.
1 - 2.54	1 - 0.40
5 - 12.70	5 - 2.00
6 - 15.24	6 - 2.40
7 - 17.78	7 - 2.80
8 - 20.32	8 - 3.20
9 - 22.86	9 - 3.50
10 - 25.40	10 - 3.90
11 - 29.94	11 - 4.30
12 - 30.48	12 - 4.70

DISTANCE

Mi. - Km.	Km. - Mi.
1 - 1.62	- 0.62
5 - 8.05	5 - 3.11
6 - 9.66	6 - 3.73
7 - 11.27	7 - 4.35
8 - 12.68	8 - 4.97
9 - 14.48	9 - 5.59
10 - 16.09	10 - 6.21
50 - 80.47	50 - 31.07
100-160.90	100 - 62.14

TEMPERATURE

P -10   0   10 20 32 40   50 60 70 8 0
90   100

C -23 -18 -12 - 7   0   4   10 16 21 27
32   38

National Eye Institute
U.S. National Institutes of Health *Research Today... Vision Tomorrow*

Eye Exams and Surgery

EyeCare America, a public service foundation of the American Academy of Ophthalmology (AAO). EyeCare America provides comprehensive eye exams and care for up to one year often at no out-of-pocket expense to eligible callers through its seniors Diabetes Eye Care Programs. Its Glaucoma Eye Care Program provides a glaucoma eye exam. The Eye Care America Children's Eye Care Program educates parents and primary care providers about the importance of early childhood (newborn through 36 months of age) eye care. Telephone: 1-800-222-EYES (3937). Website: **http://eyecareamerica.org.**

VISION USA, coordinated by the American Optometric Association (AOA), provides free eye care to uninsured, low-income workers and their families. Telephone: 1-800-766-4466. Website: **http://www.aoa.org/x5607.xml.**

Lions Clubs International provides financial assistance to individuals for eye care through local clubs. A local club can be found by using the "club locator" button found on their website at **http://www.LionsClubs.org.**

Mission Cataract USA, coordinated by the Volunteer Eye Surgeons' Association, is a program providing free cataract surgery to people of all ages who have no other means to pay. Surgeries are scheduled annually on one day, usually in May. Telephone: 1-800-343-7265. Website: **http://www.missioncataractUSA.org.**

Knights Templar Eye Foundation provides assistance for eye surgery for people who are unable to pay or receive adequate assistance from current government agencies or similar sources. Mailing address: 1000 East State Parkway, Suite I, Schaumburg, IL 60173. Telephone: (847) 490-3838. Website: **http://www.knightstemplar.org/ktef/.**

National Keratoconus Assistance Foundation provides financial support to patients who need surgical and optometric treatment for keratoconus and other corneal problems. This organization does not have a phone number available to the public. Website: **http://www.nkcaf.org.**

InfantSEE® is a public health program designed to ensure early detection of eye conditions in babies. Member optometrists provide a free comprehensive infant eye assessment to children younger than one year. Telephone: 1-888-396-3937. Website: **http://www.infantsee.org.**

Eyeglasses

Sight for Students, a Vision Service Plan (VSP) program provides eye exams and glasses to children 18 years and younger whose families cannot afford vision care. Telephone: 1-888-290-4964. Website: **http://www.sightforstudents.org/.**

New Eyes for the Needy provides vouchers for the purchase of new prescription eyeglasses. Mailing address: 549 Millburn Avenue, P.O. Box 332, Short Hills, NJ 07078-0332. Telephone: (973) 376-4903. E-mail: **neweyesfortheneedy@verizon.net**.
Website: **http://www.neweyesfortheneedy.org**

Prescription Drugs

The Medicine Program assists people to enroll in one or more of the many patient assistance programs that provide prescription medicine free-of-charge to those in need. Patients must meet the sponsor's criteria. The program is conducted in cooperation with the patient's doctor. Mailing Address: P.O. Box 4182, Poplar Bluff, MO 63902-4182. Telephone: 1-866-694-3893.
E-mail: help@themedicineprogram.com.
Website: http://www.themedicineprogram.com.

Partnership for Prescription Assistance offers a single point of access to more than 475 public and private patient assistance programs, including more than 150 programs offered by pharmaceutical companies. Telephone: 1-888-477-2669. Website: **https://www.pparx.org.**

Government Programs

Medicare Benefit for Eye Exams *for People with Diabetes* -- People with Medicare who have diabetes can get a dilated eye exam to check for diabetic eye disease. Your doctor will decide how often you need this exam. *For People at Risk for Glaucoma* -- Glaucoma is a leading cause of vision loss. People at high risk for glaucoma include those with diabetes or a family history of glaucoma, or African Americans age 50 or older. Medicare will pay for an eye exam to check for glaucoma once every 12 months. Patients must pay 20 percent of the Medicare-approved amount after the yearly Part B deductible. Telephone: 1-800-633-4227. Website: **http://www.medicare.gov.**

State Children's Health Insurance Program (SCHIP) For little or no cost, this insurance pays for doctor visits, prescription medicines, hospitalizations, and much more for children 18 years and younger. Most states also cover the cost of dental care, eye care, and medical equipment. Telephone: 1-877-543-7669. Insure Kids Now! Website: http://www.insurekidsnow.gov/states.htm.

About the Author

This is the first book ever written by Christine Ballano nee Barea, 69 years of age. She started working on computers for over 25 years ago but as time went by she constantly kept forgetting her log-ins and passwords. After several ribbings from her friends, she decided it was time to find a way to store this information that would be readily accessible. Along came the idea to create a book that could store all this information and more to share with her friends.

She has Bachelor of Science Degree in Business Administration, a Paralegal and Office Manager for Seniors vs. Crime where she volunteers 50 percent of her time devoted to helping Seniors who have come across some unscrupulous scam artists or abusive families, friends or children. In addition to her volunteer work; she works   part-time, finds time to make jewelry, sell on EBay, go to Art Gallery openings, and attend foreign films once a month, travel, ballroom dancing and of course entertaining friends. She is the mother of two; her son Marc Ian Schnoll and her daughter Denise Timmons and four grand-daughters (Crystal, Tiffany, Tara, Paige and soon to be great-grandmother.)

www.ingramcontent.com/pod-product-compliance
Lightning Source LLC
Chambersburg PA
CBHW071217050326
40689CB00011B/2351